W9-AAR-814

Finger Knitting FOR KIDS

SUPER CUTE & EASY THINGS TO MAKE

TUTTLE Publishing

Tokyo | Rutland, Vermont | Singapore

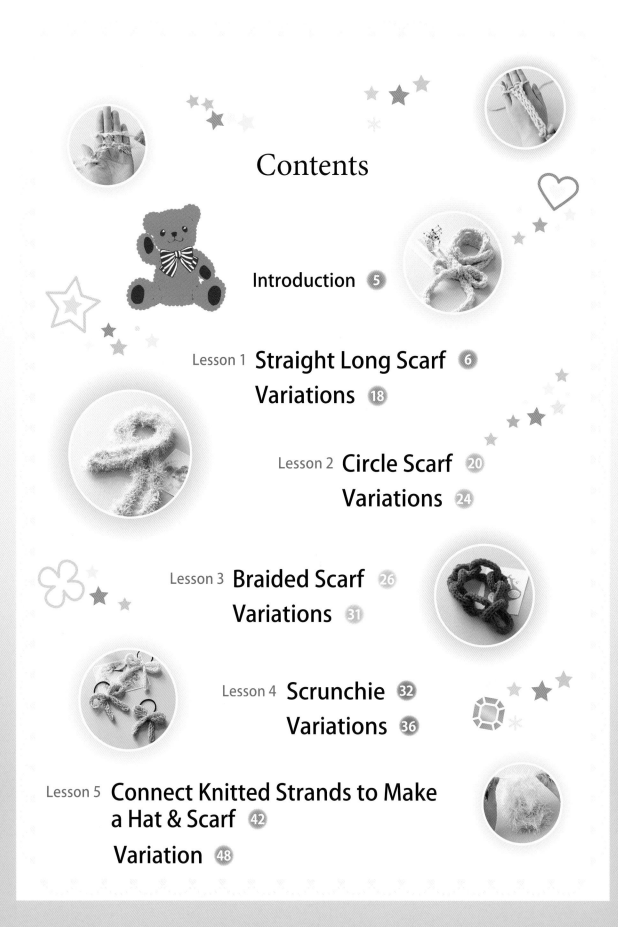

Contents

Projects

Introduction

"Knitting is so hard!" Have you ever thought that?
Even if you've never tried it before, no problem! Finger knitting is super easy!
Simple, straight stitches turn into a scarf or a scrunchie in a flash!
Connect finger knitted strands to make a hat or bag!
It's amazingly easy to create a lot of different things.
More than anything, finger knitting is fun, so let's give it a go!

Straight Long Scarf

Watch your stitches grow longer and longer with this
basic finger knitting technique and before you know it,
you'll have a scarf. Choose your favorite yarn type and colors!
Choose the length of the scarf! Let's knit!

Finger knitting is
REALLY easy. Once you
learn the steps, you just
repeat them over and over.
So much fun!

Let's start with a long scarf!

Materials **Yarn:** We used Hamanaka Lala in Dark Pink (50g). Use any extra-bulky yarn you like.

First…

All you need is yarn. Let's start by preparing the yarn. We recommend a thicker yarn weight ("yarn weight" refers to its thickness) for beginners.

Yarn with Varying Thickness

This type of yarn is thinner in some parts and thicker in others or may have uneven textures. Although it's a little trickier to use than regular smoother yarn, the stitches aren't as visible, which produces a nice finish.

Smooth Yarn

Smooth yarn has fewer bumps and textures and is easier to handle. Try selecting a thicker yarn weight. Look for ones labeled "bulky" or "chunky." You could also knit two strands of worsted or medium weight yarn together.

Prepare about 50 grams of yarn for the straight long scarf.

Let's Knit!

First, make an *oyasumi* card.
[*oyasumi* means "rest"]
Once you start knitting, you'll need to keep the yarn on your fingers. Whenever you need a break, an *oyasumi* card comes in handy. You just transfer the yarn to the card while you rest, and then pick up where you left off.

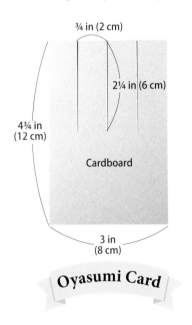

¾ in (2 cm)

2¼ in (6 cm)

4¾ in (12 cm)

Cardboard

3 in (8 cm)

Oyasumi Card

How to Transfer Yarn

Start by removing the yarn from your index finger.

Transfer the yarn to the card. Repeat with the other digits from the middle finger to pinky finger.

Finding the Yarn End

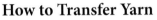

1 Insert your index finger and thumb into the center hollow of the skein and look for the end of the yarn.

2 Pull out a small ball of yarn, including the yarn end.

3 Find the yarn end.

You're all ready to begin!

Let's cast on!

1 Wrap the yarn around your thumb

Place yarn between your thumb and index finger.

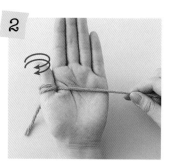

Wrap the yarn around your thumb.

Wrap twice

START ♥

2 Cast the yarn on fingers, up to the pinky finger

Bring the yarn on top of the index finger.

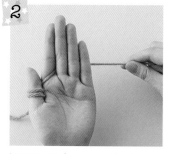

Insert yarn between the index and middle fingers.

Bring the yarn up between the middle and ring fingers.

Insert yarn behind the pinky finger.

$\mathcal{3}$ Wrap around pinky finger and reverse

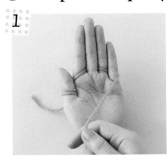

1 Wrap yarn around pinky finger.

2 Hook the yarn around the pinky, then insert behind ring finger.

3 Bring the yarn up between the ring and middle fingers.

4 Wrap yarn around middle finger and pull yarn back.

5 Bring yarn up between index finger and thumb.

You've cast on successfully!

Now that you've cast on the yarn, the rest is easy-peasy! Let's get knitting!

Finger knitting in action!

4 Pull the yarn from the skein (not the tail) across the front of your fingers

1

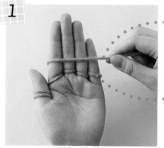

★ New yarn

Cast on yarn as shown previously.

Pull the yarn across the front of your fingers at a position slightly higher than the cast on yarn.

Since you'll be pulling "fresh" yarn across your fingers, you'll be able to knit continuously.

5 Let's knit the first stitch

1

Slightly pull up the yarn wrapped around your index finger.

2

Bend your index finger.

3

Slide the wrapped yarn over the index finger.

4

Move the yarn all the way back.

5

Pull the yarn between your fingers to tighten the stitch.

6 Repeat the steps up to the pinky finger

1

Slightly pull up the yarn wrapped around your middle finger.

2

Bend your middle finger.

3

Slide the wrapped yarn over the middle finger, all the way to the back.

4

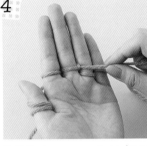

Pull the loose yarn to tighten stitch.

5

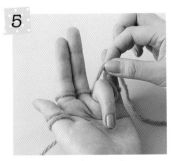

Repeat with the ring finger and slide yarn over and to the back.

6

Pull the loose yarn, and you've knitted a stitch.

7

Repeat with the pinky finger, bringing the yarn over and back.

8

Pull the loose yarn to knit the pinky stitch

Congrats! You've knitted a whole row!

7 Keep repeating previous steps to knit

1

Pull the yarn towards the back.

2

Wrap around the front of the index finger.

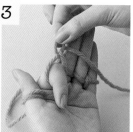

3

Start knitting from the index finger.

4

Knit up to the pinky finger.

8 Remove yarn from thumb

1

Back

Remove yarn from thumb.

Once removed, it should look like this.

2

Pull the yarn to tighten stitches.

9 Pull the yarn as you knit

1

Bring the yarn around the front.

2

Slide the yarn over and to the back to knit.

3

Knit up to the pinky finger.

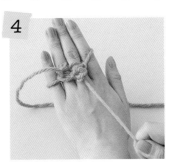

4

Once you've completed a row, pull the yarn at the back.

By pulling the yarn at the back with each row completion, the stitches will even out and will produce a nice finish.

10 rows complete!

1.1 yards [1 meter] complete!

Taking a break.

Knit as long as you want

Shown: 2¾ yd (2 m 50 cm) with 50 g yarn.

❦ How to join yarn ❦

1

Knit to the edge.

2

Tie another piece of yarn.

3

Continue knitting and tuck the knot inside a stitch to hide it.

4

The knot is not visible.

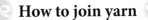

10 Let's finish the edges

1

Once you're done knitting, leave a yarn tail of about 10 in [25 cm] and cut.

2

Wrap the yarn around the back, holding the yarn end.

3

Insert the yarn under the index finger stitch.

4

Pull the yarn.

5

Insert the yarn under the middle finger stitch.

6

Repeat with the ring and pinky finger stitches.

7

Remove yarn from fingers.

8

Pull the yarn to tighten, and you're all done!

11 Let's weave in the ends

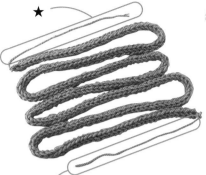

★ We will weave in this section.

1 Place a piece of tape at the yarn end.

2 Wrap the tape around and around.

3 The yarn end with wrapped tape (this is to harden the end into a "needle")

4 Insert the tape-wrapped end right by where the tail is coming out.

5 Pull out the wrapped end about 1½–2 in (4–5 cm) from the insertion point.

6 Cut the yarn.

All done!

Yay!!
I finished!
It's so warm!

Straight Long Scarf Variations

This scarf can be whipped up in less than an hour!
For optimal results, make sure to pull the yarn evenly
as you knit and have fun!

Materials

Yarn: We used Hamanaka Poco in Pink 50g. Use any super-bulky eyelash yarn you like.

Straight Long Scarf Variations

Knit with two strands together. This technique is best when using thinner yarn.

See pages 9–17 for instructions.

Materials

Yarn: We used Hamanaka Warmmy in Navy (50g). Use any medium weight yarn you like.

Materials

Yarn: We used Hamanaka Sonomono Slub in White 50g. Use any super-bulky yarn you like.

Circle Scarf

Knit a few short strands, link them together
and what do you get? A circle scarf!
The links fit nicely into each other so short
strands work well for this cute little neck warmer.

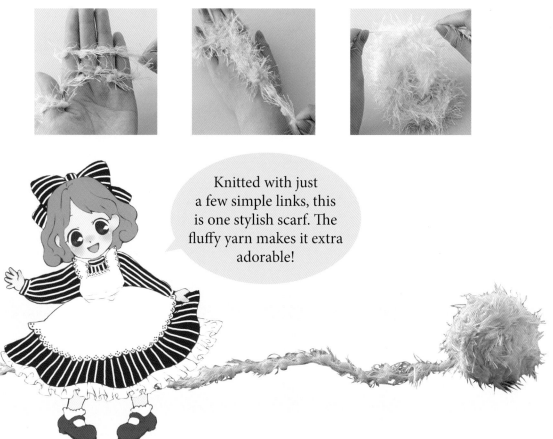

Knitted with just
a few simple links, this
is one stylish scarf. The
fluffy yarn makes it extra
adorable!

Let's make the circle scarf on page 20

Knit a bunch of short strands, form them into rings and link them together to make this voluminous, cute and warm scarf!

Materials

Yarn: We used Hamanaka Poco in Blue (20g) and White (15g). Use any super-bulky eyelash yarn you like.

1 Knit strands that are 7 in (18 cm) in length (See pages 10–17 for reference)

Cast on yarn.

Knit.

Pull yarn at back.

Knit to 7 in (18 cm) in length, remove from fingers, finish edges and pull yarn tail to secure.

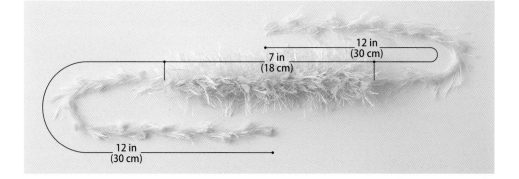

12 in (30 cm)

7 in (18 cm)

12 in (30 cm)

2 Knit 7 strands of the same length

Blue 4 strands

White 3 strands

3 Make a ring

1

2

3

4

Tie the yarn tails together and form a ring.

Tie twice.

Wrap tape around the ends and weave them in (see page 17 for reference).

The ring is complete.

4 Link the rings together

1

2

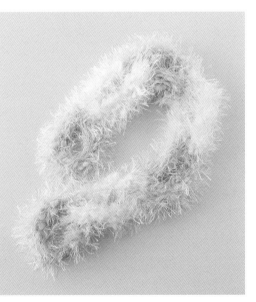

Insert a white strand into a blue ring.

Tie the yarn tails together.

3

4

Weave in the ends.

Link the next strand.

Link together 7 rings and you're all done!

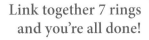

Circle Scarf Variations

The circle is so darling!

The circle is so useful!

This stylish scarf is simple because it's made of circles!

Might be even cuter if it's longer!

See pages 22–23 for instructions

Materials

Yarn: We used Hamanaka Poco in Blue (20g) and White (15g).
Use any super-bulky eyelash yarn you like.

See pages 22–23 for
instructions, and make 9 rings.

Materials

Yarn: We used Hamanaka Pom Beans in Red. (30g) Use any lightweight yarn you like.

Knit with two strands of yarn
together.

Materials

Yarn: We used Hamanaka Lala in Pink (25g) and White (20g).
Use any extra-bulky yarn you like.

Braided Scarf

This scarf is made from three long strands that are braided.
Attach a pom pom on each end for extra kawaii!
Have fun coming up with different color combinations,
including the pom pom color!

Let's make the braided scarf on page 26

For this scarf, we'll be knitting three long strands to braid together. Even if you're not familiar with braiding, using three colors will make keeping track a cinch.

Materials

Yarn: We used Hamanaka Lala in Pink (40g), White (95g) and Light Brown (40g). Use any extra-bulky yarn you like.

1 Knit strands that are about 2 yd (2 m) in length (See pages 10–17 for reference)

Cast on yarn.

Knit.

Pull yarn at back.

Knit to 2 yd (2 m) in length, remove from fingers, finish edges and pull yarn to secure.

2 Knit two more strands of the same length

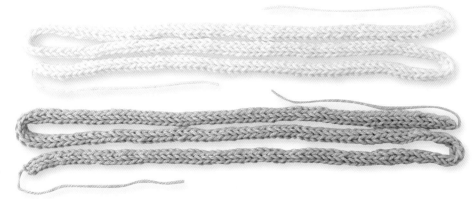

3 Braid the three strands

Tie two strands together.

Tie the third strand.

Bring the right strand (light brown) to the center.

Bring the left strand (pink) to the center.

Bring the right strand (white) to the center.

Braid loosely.

Repeat previous steps to braid.

Once you reach the end, tie two strands together.

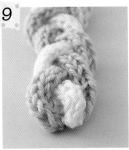

Tie the third strand.

Weave in the ends.

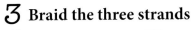

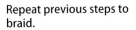

29

4 Let's make a pom pom

Make a pom pom card

Cardboard

1¼ in (3.5 cm)

3½ in (9 cm)

¾ in (2 cm)

3½ in (9 cm)

1¼ in (3.5 cm)

4¾ in (12 cm)

1

Begin wrapping the yarn around the card.

2

Wrap 120 times.

3

Thread another piece of yarn (15¾ in [40 cm]) from behind and through the center opening and tie at the center.

4

Flip the card around and tie again at the back.

5

Cut the yarn loops at the top and bottom.

6

Trim to shape into a sphere.

7

Wrap tape around the yarn ends.

Trim to about (3 in [8 cm]) in diameter.

5 Attach pom pom

1

Thread the tape-wrapped end of the pom pom yarn into the edge of scarf.

2

Tie the yarn.

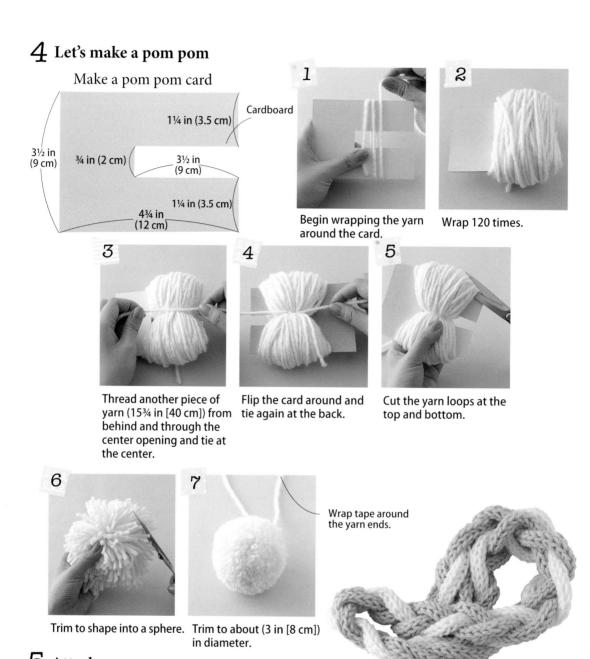

Play around with different
color combinations.
It's best to loosely braid the strands.
If you're using fluffy yarn, consider
omitting the pom poms.

See pages 28–30 for instructions.

Materials

Yarn: We used Hamanaka Poco in Pink (40g), White (40g)
and Cream (40g). Use any super-bulky eyelash yarn you like.

Materials

Yarn: We used Hamanaka Lala in Pink (40g), Light Pink (95g)
and Purple (40g). Use any extra-bulky yarn you like.

Scrunchie

All you need to do is include the hair tie while knitting!
Scrunchie-making is so quick and easy, you'll want to
make lots and hand them out as gifts.
This sweet accessory is sure to be a hit!

Let's make the scrunchie on page 32

By inserting the elastic hair tie while knitting, this delightful accessory can be made oh-so-easily. The technique of including the elastic is simply brilliant!

Materials

Yarn: We used Hamanaka Lala in Orange, Pink, Red, Blue and Yellow Green (7g each). Use any extra-bulky yarn you like.

Hair Tie: (black) one piece

1 Make a yarn ball

Wrap yarn around hand.

Once you've wrapped the yarn a few times, remove from your hand and continue wrapping the yarn.

Keep wrapping the yarn into a ball of about 7g.

2 Insert elastic while knitting

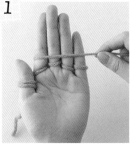

Cast on yarn (see pages 10–13 for reference).

Knit up to the pinky finger to complete the first row.

Insert the yarn ball through the elastic hair tie.

4

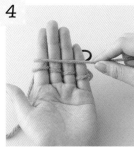 

Wrap the yarn around on top of your fingers.

[Back]

5

Knit up to the pinky finger to complete the second row.

6

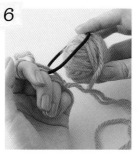

Insert the yarn ball through the elastic hair tie.

7

Repeat knitting a row then inserting the yarn ball through the elastic hair tie until you run out of yarn.

8

Finish edge and remove from your hand. Pull the yarn to tighten and secure.

Make sure to insert the yarn ball through the hair tie as you knit each row.

3 Weave in ends

1

Tie the yarn tails twice.

2

Wrap the yarn ends with tape and weave in (see page 17 for reference)

3

Trim extra yarn.

All done!

Scrunchie Variations

Look how cute these fluffy scrunchies are!
How about wearing them on your wrists
for added warmth?

See pages 34–35 for instructions.

Materials

Yarn: We used Hamanaka Poco in Pink, Dark Pink, White, and Orange (7g each).
Use any super-bulky eyelash yarn you like.

Hair Tie: (black) one piece

 Materials

Yarn: We used Hamanaka Poco in Yellow, Green, Blue, and
Light Blue (7g each). Use any super-bulky eyelash yarn
you like.

Hair Tie: (black) one piece

Scrunchie Variations

Ribbon Scrunchie
Tie the strand into a cute bow!

See page 40 for instructions

Flower Scrunchie
Use a slightly thinner yarn to knit into a flower shape!

See page 41 for instructions

A great gift idea!

Let's make the ribbon scrunchie on page 38

The key point for this ribbon scrunchie is to keep the stitches small. Select your favorite yarn colors to knit these up.

Materials

Yarn: We used Hamanaka Pom Beans in Blue, Yellow and Pink (4g each). Use any lightweight yarn you like.
Hair Tie: (black) one piece

1 Knit to 15¾ in (40 cm) in length (See pages 10–17 for reference)

2 Attach the ribbon

1

2

3

4

Wrap tape around the yarn tail ends, weave them into the knitted strand and cut off excess.

Finish both edges.

Insert into hair tie.

Tie in the middle.

5

Tie into a bow.

All done!

Let's make the flower scrunchie on page 39

The petals are formed by looping the strands. Super easy! A thinner yarn weight is recommended.

Materials

Yarn: We used Hamanaka Pom Beans in Red, Orange, Blue (4g each). Use any lightweight yarn you like.

Hair Tie: (black) one piece

1 Knit to 15¾ in (40 cm) in length
(See pages 10–17 for reference)

2 Create the flower shape

Tie the yarn tails twice.

Measure about 3 in (8 cm) of the loop and tie off to form a flower petal.

Repeat to make five petals and tie the yarn twice on the backside.

Tie onto the hair tie twice.

Wrap tape on the yarn tail ends and weave in, cutting off the excess.

All done!

Connect Knitted Strands
to Make a Hat & Scarf

Decide on a particular length, knit about four or five strands to
that length and connect them together to make a wider scarf.

Let's make the tassel scarf on page 42

Knit a few long strands and connect them together side-by-side. It's easy to do! Wrap tape around the tail ends to make them into "needles" and carefully adjoin the strands.

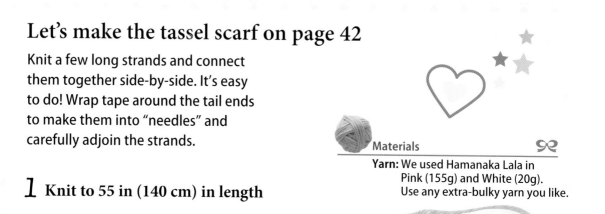

Materials ❧

Yarn: We used Hamanaka Lala in Pink (155g) and White (20g). Use any extra-bulky yarn you like.

1 Knit to 55 in (140 cm) in length

2 Connect two knitted strands

1

Tightly wrap tape on the tail end of the strand that will be attached. This will create a "needle" out of the tail end.

2

1 Tie the tape-wrapped yarn from step 1 to the other strand's tail, at the top (where the knitting ends).

3

Align the two strands and insert the "needle" diagonally and scoop up a stitch.

4

Pull the yarn taut and insert the "needle" diagonally above the previous stitch.

5

Repeat until the two knitted strands are completely connected.

[Front]

3 Let's connect 5 knitted strands

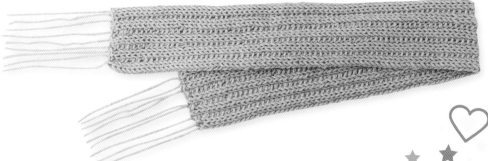

4 Let's finish the edges and attach the tassels

Prepare the cardboard.

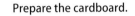

4¾ in
(12 cm)   Cardboard

4 in
(10 cm)

1 Wrap tape around tail end and weave in. Then trim excess yarn.

2 Weave in all the loose yarn.

3 Wrap yarn around the cardboard 54 times.

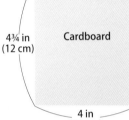

4 Cut only one side.

5 Make a tool out of a piece of 8 in (20 cm) by wrapping tape on both tail ends.

6 Place three strands of cut yarn on the tool from previous step.

7 Starting at the corner edge, insert one end of the tool.

8 Form a loop with the attached yarn and pull the yarn ends through the loop.

9 Pull the ends to secure. Now you're created one tassel.

10 Attach 9 tassels and even out the ends by trimming to about 4 in (10 cm).

All done!

45

Let's make the pom pom hat on page 42

This hat uses the same technique as the tassel scarf to connect the knitted strands. Opt for the same yarn as the scarf for a pulled-together look and top this cutie off with some pom poms!

Materials

Yarn: We used Hamanaka Lala in Pink (80g) and White (20g). Use any extra-bulky yarn you like.

1 **Knit 7 strands that are 19¾ in (50 cm) in length**
(See pages 10–17 for reference)

2 **Connect the 7 knitted strands**
(See pages 44–45 for reference)

Tie the yarn tails on each sides together to shape the hat.

3 **Connect to create a circular shape**

Starting at the bottom, tie the corresponding yarn tails from each side together.

Continue tying all the way up the sides.

3

Leave one tail at the top and bottom alone, wrap tape on the tail ends for the rest and weave them in.

4

Wrap a long piece of tape on the bottom tail end.

5

Use the taped yarn to whip stitch the sides together.

4 Let's close the top

1

Tie a 23½ in (60 cm) piece of yarn to the remaining top yarn.

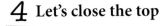

2

Wrap the yarn end of the newly attached piece with tape and whip stitch the top closed.

3

Turn right side out.

5 Let's attach the pom poms (See page 30 for reference)

Make the pom pom card

Cardboard

¾ in (2 cm)

2 in (5 cm)   ½ in (1 cm)   2 in (5 cm)

3 in (8 cm)   ¾ in (2 cm)

1

1½ in (4 cm)

Make the pom pom (wrap yarn around card 50 times).

2

Thread one of the pom pom tail ends into the upper corner of the hat.

3

Tie tightly.

4

Attach 2 pom poms per side.

All done!

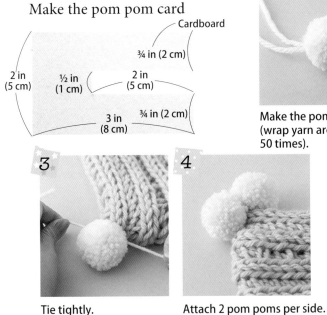

Pom Pom Hat Variation

Repeat the steps for the pom pom hat and add a heart! The simple knitted heart is made from a single strand. You'll want to make a bevy of them for friends!

Let's make a heart hat

Materials ✄

Yarn: We used—For the pink hat: Hamanaka Lala in Dark Pink
(80g), White (30g) and Purple (20g).
For the blue hat: Hamanaka Lala in Light Blue (80g)
White (30g) Blue (20g). Use any extra-bulky yarn you like.

Finished size ✄

Circumference: 19¾ in (50 cm)
Depth: 6¼ in (16 cm)

1 Make the hat

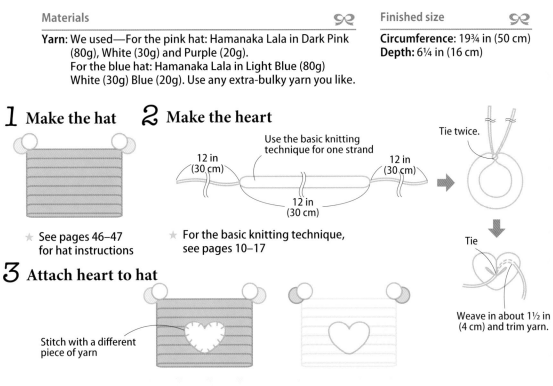

★ See pages 46–47
for hat instructions

2 Make the heart

Use the basic knitting
technique for one strand

12 in
(30 cm)

12 in
(30 cm)

12 in
(30 cm)

Tie twice.

Tie

Weave in about 1½ in
(4 cm) and trim yarn.

★ For the basic knitting technique,
see pages 10–17

3 Attach heart to hat

Stitch with a different
piece of yarn

Tricolor hat

Lengthen the hat, gather the top and attach a pom pom! You'll want to wear this stylish tricolor hat over and over!

Let's make a tricolor hat

Materials ✿

Yarn: We used Hamanaka Warmmy in Navy (105g), Red (25g) and White (10g). Use any medium weight yarn you like.

Finished size ✿

Circumference: 19¾ in (50 cm)
Depth: 9 in (23 cm)

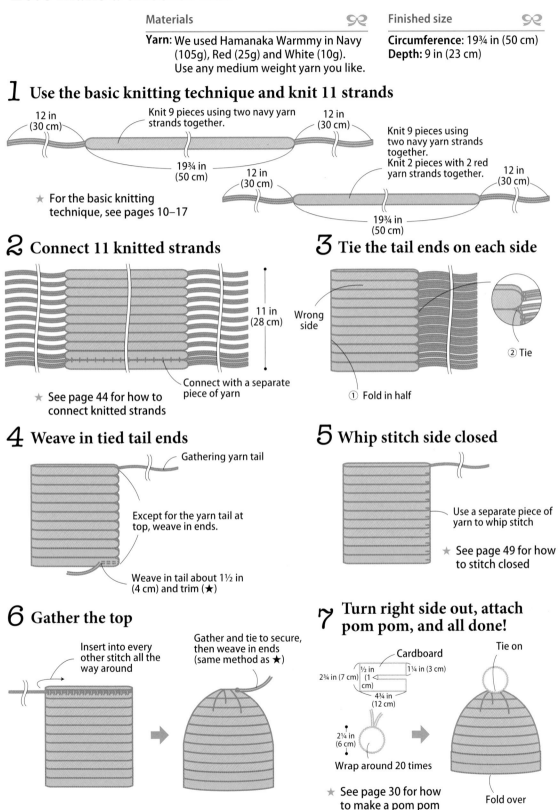

1 Use the basic knitting technique and knit 11 strands

12 in (30 cm)

Knit 9 pieces using two navy yarn strands together.

12 in (30 cm)

19¾ in (50 cm)

★ For the basic knitting technique, see pages 10–17

Knit 9 pieces using two navy yarn strands together. Knit 2 pieces with 2 red yarn strands together.

12 in (30 cm)

12 in (30 cm)

19¾ in (50 cm)

2 Connect 11 knitted strands

11 in (28 cm)

Connect with a separate piece of yarn

★ See page 44 for how to connect knitted strands

3 Tie the tail ends on each side

Wrong side

② Tie

① Fold in half

4 Weave in tied tail ends

Gathering yarn tail

Except for the yarn tail at top, weave in ends.

Weave in tail about 1½ in (4 cm) and trim (★)

5 Whip stitch side closed

Use a separate piece of yarn to whip stitch

★ See page 49 for how to stitch closed

6 Gather the top

Insert into every other stitch all the way around

Gather and tie to secure, then weave in ends (same method as ★)

7 Turn right side out, attach pom pom, and all done!

Cardboard

Tie on

2¾ in (7 cm)

½ in (1 cm)

1¼ in (3 cm)

4¾ in (12 cm)

2¼ in (6 cm)

Wrap around 20 times

★ See page 30 for how to make a pom pom

Fold over

Striped Purse

A few braids quickly transform into this mini bag.
Have fun choosing your favorite color combinations!

Let's Try
Finger Knitting
Lesson 2

Let's Make a Striped Purse

Materials ❧

Yarn: We used Hamanaka Lala in Dark Pink (35g) Orange and Yellow Green (7g each). Use any extra-bulky yarn you like.

Finished size ❧

Circumference: 6¼ in (16 cm)
Depth: 7 in (18 cm)
Shoulder strap length: 37 in (94 cm)

1 Knit 7 strands using the basic technique

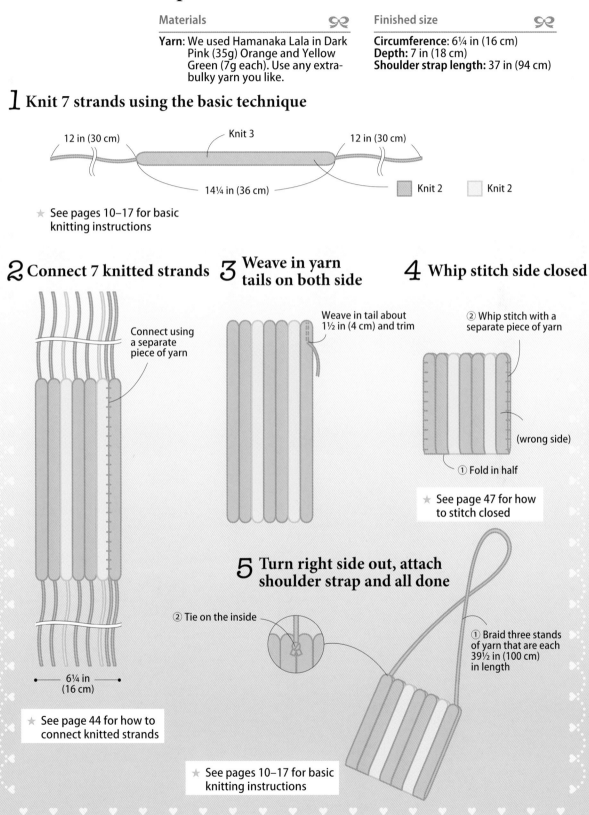

12 in (30 cm)

Knit 3

12 in (30 cm)

14¼ in (36 cm)

Knit 2   Knit 2

★ See pages 10–17 for basic knitting instructions

2 Connect 7 knitted strands

Connect using a separate piece of yarn

6¼ in (16 cm)

★ See page 44 for how to connect knitted strands

3 Weave in yarn tails on both side

Weave in tail about 1½ in (4 cm) and trim

4 Whip stitch side closed

② Whip stitch with a separate piece of yarn

(wrong side)

① Fold in half

★ See page 47 for how to stitch closed

5 Turn right side out, attach shoulder strap and all done

② Tie on the inside

① Braid three stands of yarn that are each 39½ in (100 cm) in length

★ See pages 10–17 for basic knitting instructions

Magic Scrubber

Knit a long strand out of acrylic yarn and tie it here and there to make a flower-shaped or round scrubber. It's a great gift idea too!

Let's make a magic scrubber

Materials	❦	Finished size	❦

Yarn: We used Hamanaka Bonny in Pink, Orange (20g each) Blue, Light Blue (15g each). Use any bulky yarn you like.

Circumference: 6¼ in (16 cm)
Depth: 5½ in (14 cm)

1 Knit one strand using the basic technique

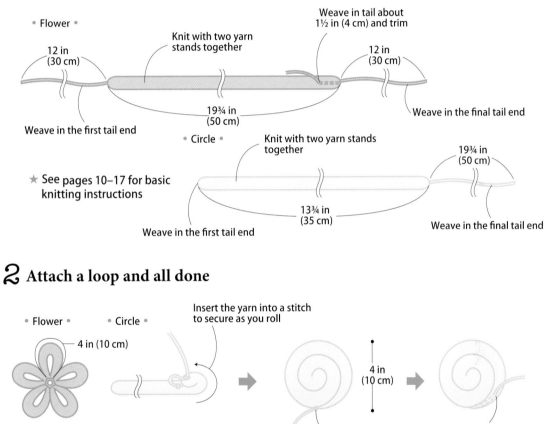

• Flower •

12 in (30 cm)

Knit with two yarn stands together

Weave in tail about 1½ in (4 cm) and trim

12 in (30 cm)

19¾ in (50 cm)

Weave in the first tail end

Weave in the final tail end

★ See pages 10–17 for basic knitting instructions

• Circle •

Knit with two yarn stands together

19¾ in (50 cm)

13¾ in (35 cm)

Weave in the first tail end

Weave in the final tail end

2 Attach a loop and all done

• Flower •   • Circle •

4 in (10 cm)

Insert the yarn into a stitch to secure as you roll

4 in (10 cm)

Tie

Weave in tail about 1½ in (4 cm) and trim

★ See page 41 for how to make a flower

3 Attach a loop and all done

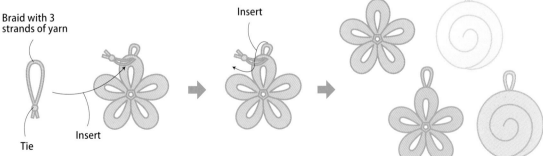

Braid with 3 strands of yarn

Tie

Insert

Insert

Blue Pillow

Connecting a bunch of knitted strands makes for an adorable pillow. Change up the colors to form stripes and/or add pom poms!

Let's Try
Finger Knitting
Lesson 4

Let's make a blue pillow

Materials ✂

Yarn: We used Hamanaka Bonny in Light Blue (15g) and Blue (25g). Use any bulky yarn you like.

Finished size ✂

Height: 12½ in (32 cm)
Width: 12½ in (32 cm)

1 Knit 13 strands using the basic technique

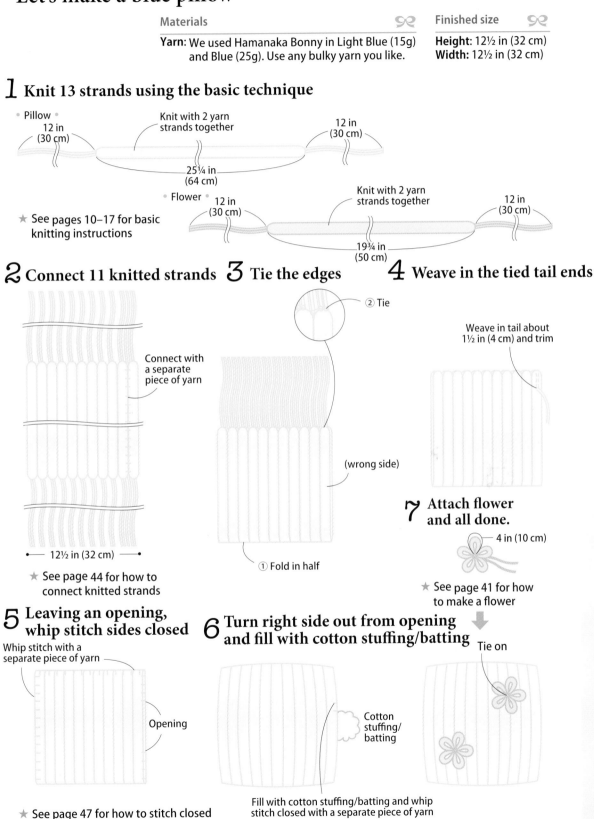

• Pillow •
12 in (30 cm)

Knit with 2 yarn strands together

12 in (30 cm)

25¼ in (64 cm)

• Flower •
12 in (30 cm)

Knit with 2 yarn strands together

12 in (30 cm)

19¾ in (50 cm)

★ See pages 10–17 for basic knitting instructions

2 Connect 11 knitted strands

Connect with a separate piece of yarn

12½ in (32 cm)

★ See page 44 for how to connect knitted strands

3 Tie the edges

② Tie

(wrong side)

① Fold in half

4 Weave in the tied tail ends

Weave in tail about 1½ in (4 cm) and trim

7 Attach flower and all done.

4 in (10 cm)

★ See page 41 for how to make a flower

5 Leaving an opening, whip stitch sides closed

Whip stitch with a separate piece of yarn

Opening

★ See page 47 for how to stitch closed

6 Turn right side out from opening and fill with cotton stuffing/batting

Tie on

Cotton stuffing/batting

Fill with cotton stuffing/batting and whip stitch closed with a separate piece of yarn

Flower Floor Cushion

Knit an extra, extra long strand, roll it
up, and voila! A flower floor cushion.
You can place it on a chair too!

Let's make a flower floor cushion

Materials

Yarn: We used Hamanaka Bonny in Yellow (85g) and Orange 20g. Use any bulky yarn you like.

Finished size

Diameter: 13 in (33 cm)

1 Knit 2 strands using the basic technique

Flower center •

Knit with 2 yarn strands together

15¾ in (40 cm)

Weave in the first tail end

78¾ in (200 cm)

Weave in final tail end

★ See pages 10–17 for basic knitting instructions

• Flower petal •

12 in (30 cm)

Knit with 2 yarn strands together

12 in (30 cm)

Weave in the first tail end

41 in (104 cm)

Weave in final tail end

2 Make the flower center

Insert tail end into a stitch to secure as you roll the strand

● If you run out of yarn, tie on an additional piece of yarn.

10 in (25 cm)

Tie

Weave in tail about 1½ in (4 cm) and trim

3 Make the petals

② Make 8 evenly-placed connections.

5 in (13 cm)

① Tie on

59

Fluffy Lap Blanket

Knit up a number of strands in soft, fluffy yarn, connect them and the result is a comfy lap blanket! Note the sporty white stripes in this example—flex your creativity with various color combos.

Let's make a fluffy lap blanket

Materials

Yarn: We used Hamanaka Poco in Pink (275g) and Hamanaka Lala in White (80g). Use any super-bulky eyelash (pink) and extra-bulky (white) yarn you like.

Finished size

Width: 33½ in (85 cm)
Length: 19¾ in (50 cm)

1 Knit 18 strands using the basic technique

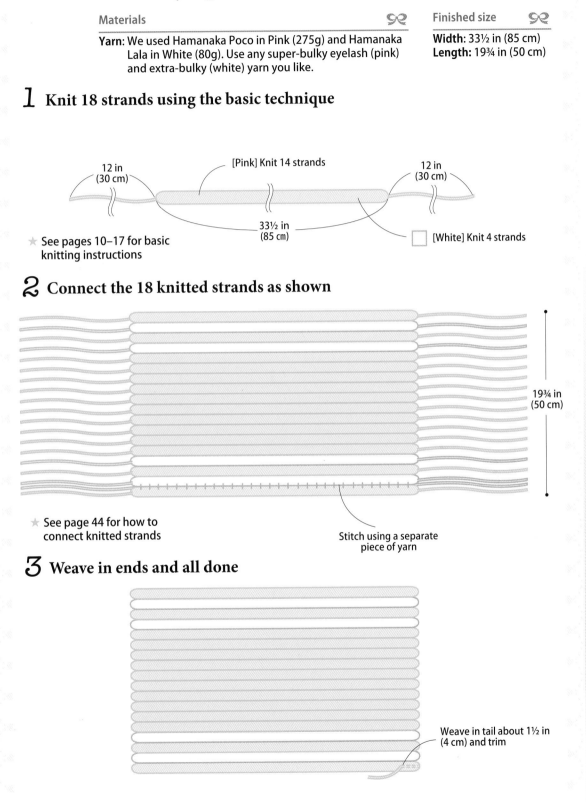

12 in (30 cm)

[Pink] Knit 14 strands

12 in (30 cm)

33½ in (85 cm)

[White] Knit 4 strands

★ See pages 10–17 for basic knitting instructions

2 Connect the 18 knitted strands as shown

19¾ in (50 cm)

★ See page 44 for how to connect knitted strands

Stitch using a separate piece of yarn

3 Weave in ends and all done

Weave in tail about 1½ in (4 cm) and trim

Perfect as a gift…

The best part of handmade is the very act of creating... Also... there's the joy of giving. Even the smallest gift, like the scrunchie, makes for a thoughtful present.

The End

Did you enjoy finger knitting?
Were you surprised by how quickly you could make a scrunchie or scarf?
As your skills develop, knitting becomes more and more fun.
Try different knitting projects beyond this book and experience the thrill of
challenging yourself to learn new skills!
We hope you've had a wonderful time making things by hand!
Make sure to infuse a lot of love into even the tiniest projects.

"Books to Span the East and West"

Tuttle Publishing was founded in 1832 in the small New England town of Rutland, Vermont (USA). Our core values remain as strong today as they were then—to publish best-in-class books which bring people together one page at a time. In 1948, we established a publishing office in Japan—and Tuttle is now a leader in publishing English-language books about the arts, languages and cultures of Asia. The world has become a much smaller place today and Asia's economic and cultural influence has grown. Yet the need for meaningful dialogue and information about this diverse region has never been greater. Over the past seven decades, Tuttle has published thousands of books on subjects ranging from martial arts and paper crafts to language learning and literature—and our talented authors, illustrators, designers and photographers have won many prestigious awards. We welcome you to explore the wealth of information available on Asia at **www.tuttlepublishing.com**.

Published by Tuttle Publishing, an imprint of Periplus Editions (HK) Ltd.

KANTAN! KAWAII! HITORI DE DEKIRU! YUBIAMI
Copyright © Eriko Teranishi 2012
English translation rights arranged Nitto Shoin Honsha Co., Ltd. through Japan UNI Agency, Inc., Tokyo

(Original Japanese edition)
Photography Tetsuya Narikiyo
Design Nexus Design / Chihiro Yano
Cover Design Cycle Design
Production Yuki Suzuki, Yukiko Muroi, Akiko Seki, Yuko Kashima
Instructional Illustrations Rin Suzuki
Illustrations Akuri Amano
Editor Kosei-sha Kainoki
Production Assistants Kaori Kaburaki (Tatsumi Publishing)

ISBN 978-4-8053-1533-0

Translated from Japanese by Sanae Ishida
English Translation ©2019 Periplus Editions (HK) Ltd.

All rights reserved. No part of this publication may be reproduced or utilized in any form or by any means, electronic or mechanical, including photocopying, recording, or by any information storage and retrieval system, without prior written permission from the publisher.

Distributed by:
North America, Latin America & Europe
Tuttle Publishing
364 Innovation Drive, North Clarendon
VT 05759-9436 U.S.A.
Tel: 1 (802) 773-8930; Fax: 1 (802) 773-6993
info@tuttlepublishing.com
www.tuttlepublishing.com

Japan
Tuttle Publishing
Yaekari Building 3rd Floor
5-4-12 Osaki Shinagawa-ku, Tokyo 141 0032
Tel: (81) 3 5437-0171; Fax: (81) 3 5437-0755
sales@tuttle.co.jp; www.tuttle.co.jp

Asia Pacific
Berkeley Books Pte. Ltd.
3 Kallang Sector, #04-01, Singapore 349278
Tel: (65) 67412178; Fax: (65) 67412179
inquiries@periplus.com.sg
www.tuttlepublishing.com

Printed in Singapore   2102TP

23 22 21   10 9 8 7 6 5 4 3

TUTTLE PUBLISHING® is a registered trademark of Tuttle Publishing, a division of Periplus Editions (HK) Ltd.